Scott Foresman

Reading
Kindergarten

Wordless Take-Home Stories

Scott Foresman

Editorial Offices: Glenview, Illinois • Parsippany, New Jersey • New York, New York
Sales Offices: Parsippany, New Jersey • Duluth, Georgia • Glenview, Illinois
Carrollton, Texas • Ontario, California

Copyright © Pearson Education, Inc.

All rights reserved. Printed in the United States of America.

The blackline masters in this publication are designed for use with
appropriate equipment to reproduce copies for classroom use only.
Scott Foresman grants permission to classroom teachers to reproduce
from these masters.

ISBN 0-328-02301-9

1 2 3 4 5 6 7 8 9 10-V039-09 08 07 06 05 04 03 02 01

Table of Contents

Who Wears a Hat?

illustrated by Lori Osiecki

Scott Foresman
Reading
Kindergarten

Kindergarten
Wordless Story 1

Who Wears a Hat?
illustrated by
Lori Osiecki

Scott Foresman

This book belongs to

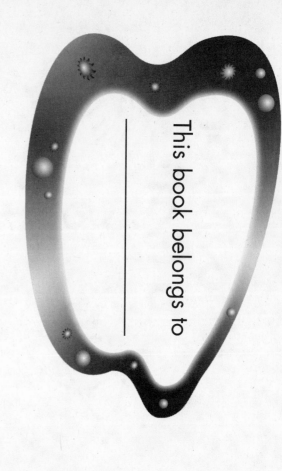

_____

Activities for Families: Encourage your child to tell a story using the illustrations in this book. Then talk about the hats you and your child wear and the activities you do when wearing each hat.

Who Wears a Hat?

illustrated by Lori Osiecki

Scott Foresman

Editorial Offices: Glenview, Illinois • Parsippany, New Jersey • New York, New York
Sales Offices: Parsippany, New Jersey • Duluth, Georgia
Glenview, Illinois • Carrollton, Texas • Ontario, California

© Scott Foresman

Happy Birthday

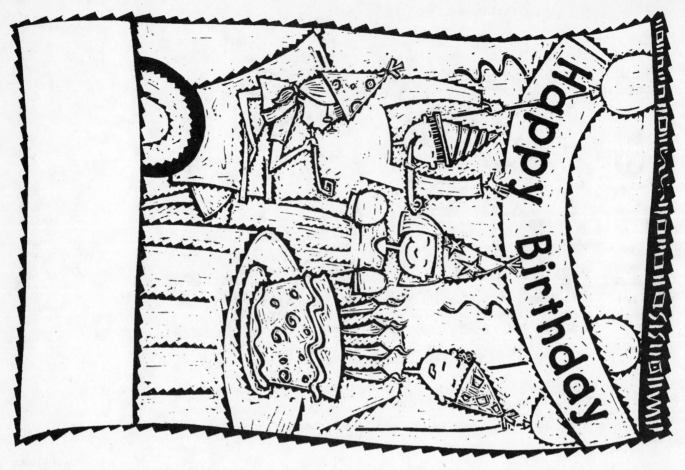

© Scott Foresman

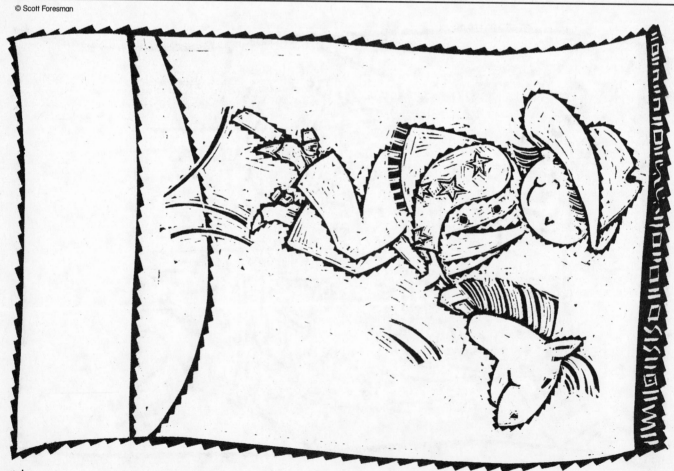

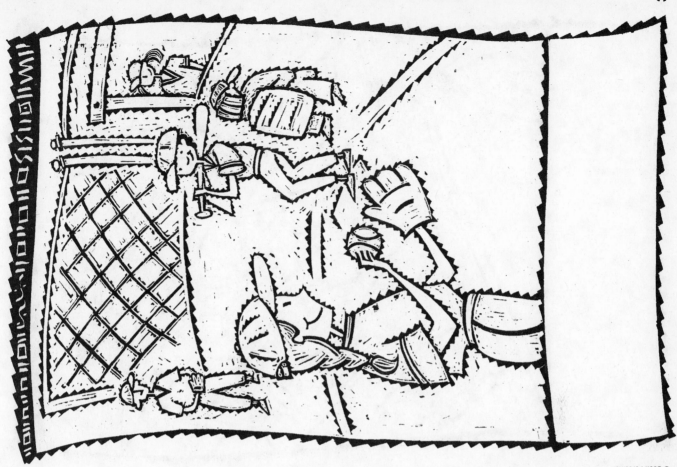

© Scott Foresman

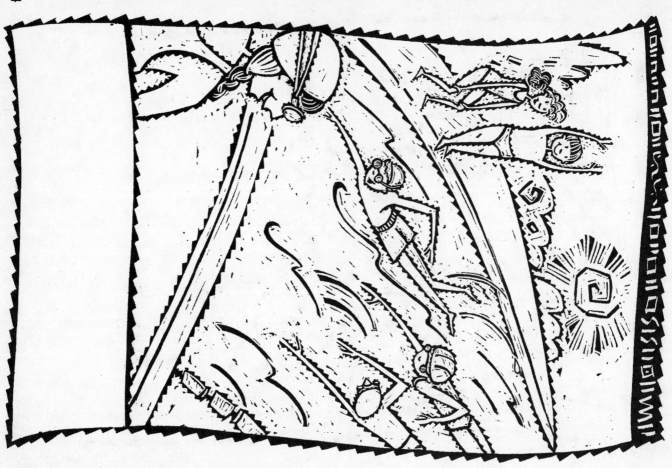

© Scott Foresman

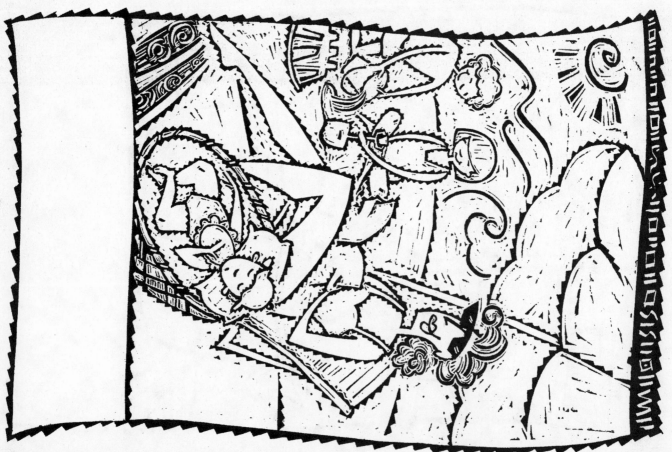

Where Is the Frog?

illustrated by Tom Garcia

Scott Foresman
Reading
Kindergarten

Kindergarten
Wordless Story 2

Where Is the Frog?
illustrated by
Tom Garcia

Scott Foresman

This book belongs to

_____

Activities for Families: Have your child use the pictures in this book to tell a story. Then invite your child to name other animals that hop.

Where Is the Frog?

illustrated by Tom Garcia

Scott Foresman

Editorial Offices: Glenview, Illinois • Parsippany, New Jersey • New York, New York
Sales Offices: Parsippany, New Jersey • Duluth, Georgia
Glenview, Illinois • Carrollton, Texas • Ontario, California

© Scott Foresman

8

© Scott Foresman

© Scott Foresman

3

6

What Can Kim Do?

illustrated by Steve Sanford

Scott Foresman Reading
Kindergarten

Kindergarten
Wordless Story 3

What Can Kim Do?
illustrated by
Steve Sanford

Scott Foresman

This book belongs to

_____

Activities for Families: Invite your child to tell a story using the pictures in this book. After sharing, encourage your child to talk about what he or she likes to do on rainy days.

What Can Kim Do?

illustrated by Steve Sanford

Scott Foresman

Editorial Offices: Glenview, Illinois • Parsippany, New Jersey • New York, New York
Sales Offices: Parsippany, New Jersey • Duluth, Georgia
Glenview, Illinois • Carrollton, Texas • Ontario, California

© Scott Foresman

© Scott Foresman

© Scott Foresman

© Scott Foresman

In the Kitchen with Nan

illustrated by Lane Yerkes

Scott Foresman Reading
Kindergarten

Kindergarten
Wordless Story 4

In the Kitchen
with Nan
illustrated by
Lane Yerkes

Scott Foresman

This book belongs to

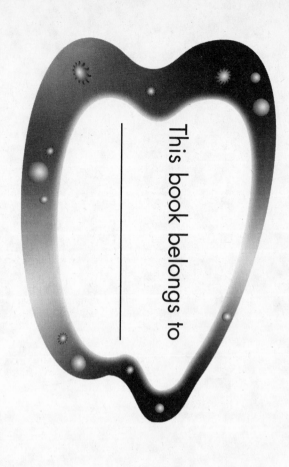

_____

Activities for Families: Have your child tell a story using the illustrations in the book. Talk about foods your child likes to make or eat.

In the Kitchen with Nan

illustrated by Lane Yerkes

Scott Foresman

Editorial Offices: Glenview, Illinois • Parsippany, New Jersey • New York, New York
Sales Offices: Parsippany, New Jersey • Duluth, Georgia
Glenview, Illinois • Carrollton, Texas • Ontario, California

© Scott Foresman

Mmm!

Mmm!

Mmm!

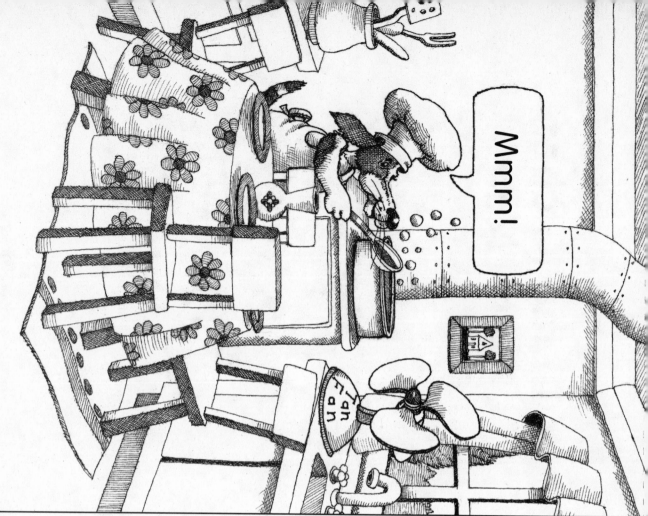

© Scott Foresman

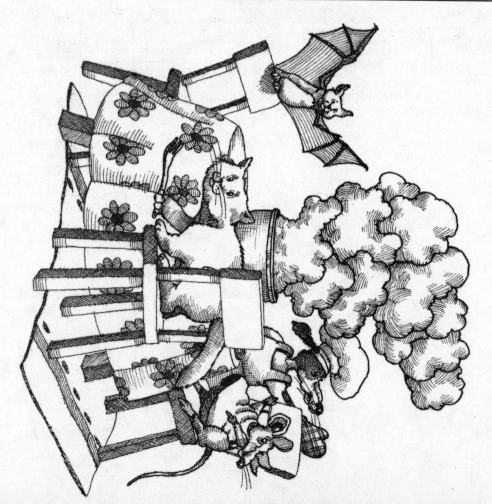

© Scott Foresman

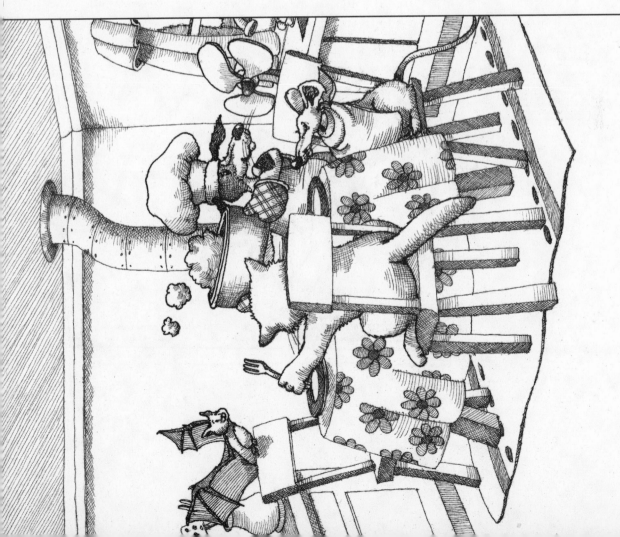

© Scott Foresman

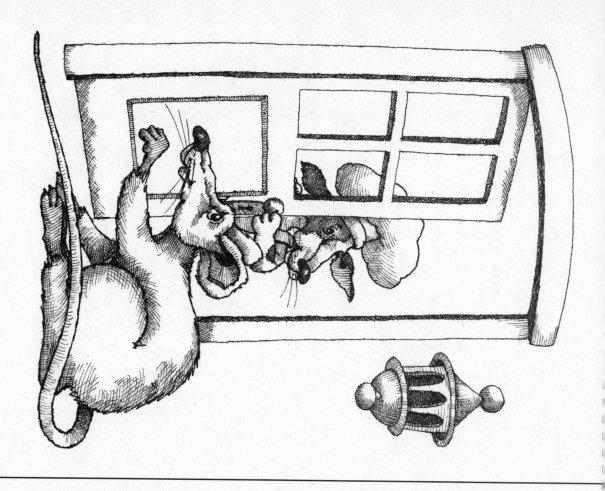

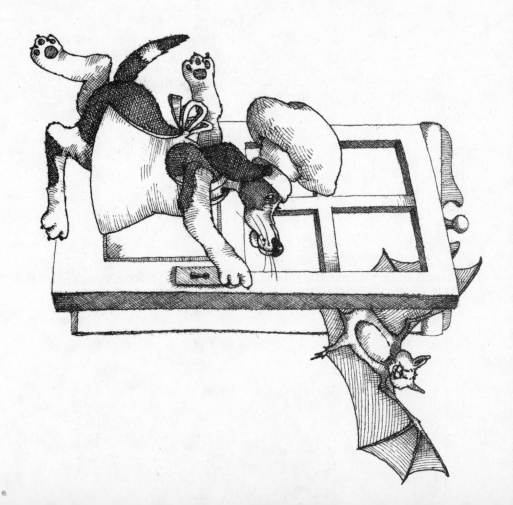

Meet My Family

illustrated by Tom Barrett

Scott Foresman Reading
Kindergarten

Kindergarten
Wordless Story 5

Meet My Family
illustrated by
Tom Barrett

Scott Foresman

This book belongs to

_____

Activities for Families: Look at the scenes in this book and encourage your child to tell a story about each one. Invite your child to talk about fun activities to do with members of your family.

Meet My Family

illustrated by Tom Barrett

Scott Foresman

Editorial Offices: Glenview, Illinois • Parsippany, New Jersey • New York, New York
Sales Offices: Parsippany, New Jersey • Duluth, Georgia
Glenview, Illinois • Carrollton, Texas • Ontario, California

© Scott Foresman

© Scott Foresman

© Scott Foresman

© Scott Foresman

ABC Stories

illustrated by Kate Flanagan

Scott Foresman Reading

Kindergarten
Wordless Story 6

ABC Stories
illustrated by
Kate Flanagan

Scott Foresman

This book belongs to

_____

Activities for Families: Look at the scenes in this book and encourage your child to tell a story about each one. Then pick a letter, go back through the book, and have your child find objects in the pictures whose names begin with that letter.

ABC Stories

illustrated by Kate Flanagan

Scott Foresman

Editorial Offices: Glenview, Illinois • Parsippany, New Jersey • New York, New York
Sales Offices: Parsippany, New Jersey • Duluth, Georgia
Glenview, Illinois • Carrollton, Texas • Ontario, California

© Scott Foresman

© Scott Foresman

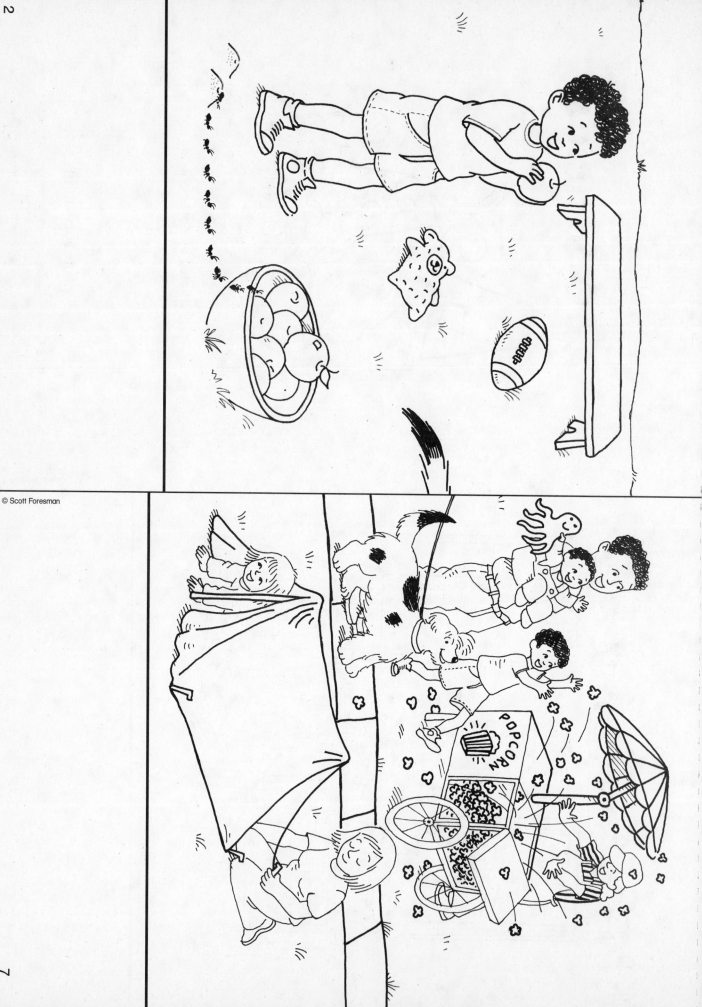

© Scott Foresman

© Scott Foresman

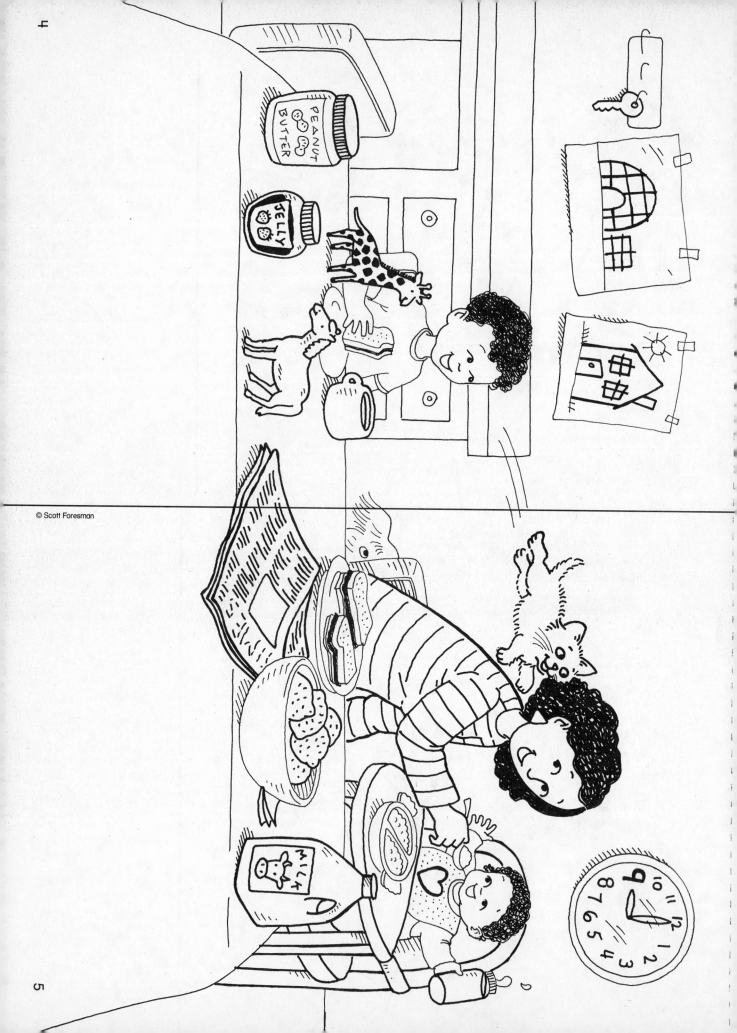

4

5

My Mitten

illustrated by Lisa Zolnowski

Scott Foresman **Reading** Kindergarten

Kindergarten
Wordless Story 7

My Mitten
illustrated by
Lisa Zolnowski

Phonics Skill:
• Initial consonant *m*

Scott Foresman

This book belongs to

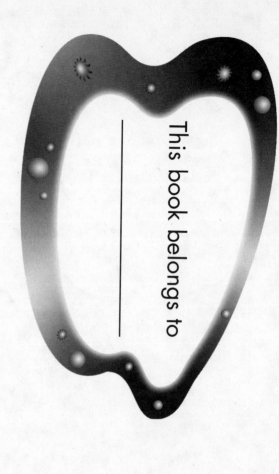

_____

Activities for Families: This book gives your child practice with words that begin with m, as in mitten. After telling the story together, help your child identify the objects in the pictures whose names begin with m.

Phonics Skill: Initial consonant m

My Mitten

illustrated by Lisa Zolnowski

Scott Foresman

Editorial Offices: Glenview, Illinois • Parsippany, New Jersey • New York, New York
Sales Offices: Parsippany, New Jersey • Duluth, Georgia
Glenview, Illinois • Carrollton, Texas • Ontario, California

© Scott Foresman

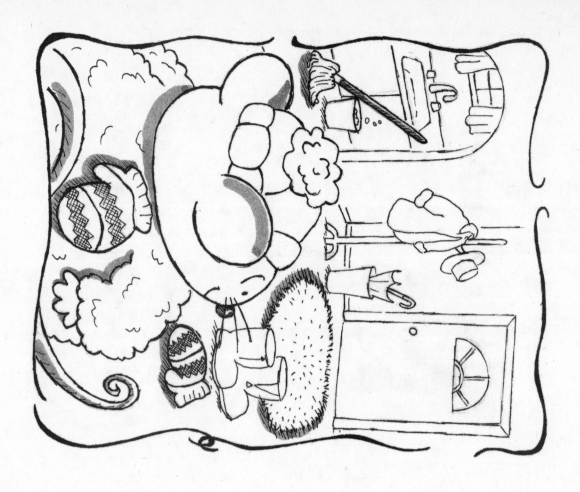

© Scott Foresman

© Scott Foresman

© Scott Foresman

Bears and Boys

Scott Foresman Reading
Kindergarten

Kindergarten
Wordless Story 8

Bears and Boys

Phonics Skill:
• Initial consonant *b*

Scott Foresman

This book belongs to

_____

Activities for Families: This book features objects that begin with _b_ as in _bears_. Share the book and then have your child point out the objects in the pictures that begin with _b_.

Phonics Skill: Initial consonant _b_

Bears and Boys

Scott Foresman

Editorial Offices: Glenview, Illinois • Parsippany, New Jersey • New York, New York
Sales Offices: Parsippany, New Jersey • Duluth, Georgia
Glenview, Illinois • Carrollton, Texas • Ontario, California

© Scott Foresman

© Scott Foresman

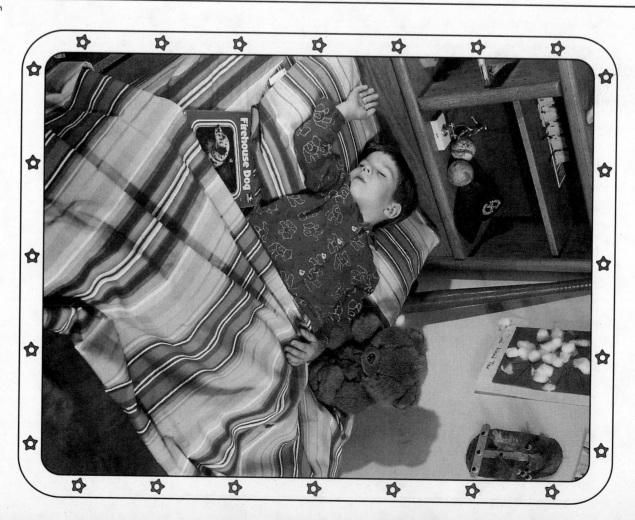

© Scott Foresman

4

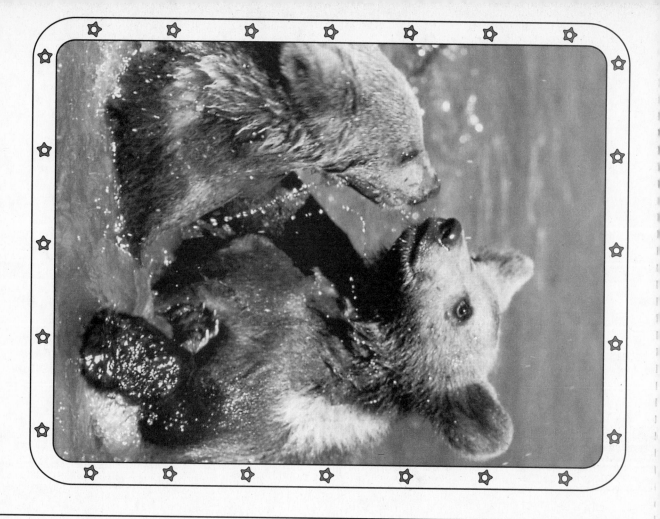

© Scott Foresman

5

Seven Sisters

Sara 6
Sally 4
Sukie 3
Sofie 5
Sandy 2
Sonia 1

illustrated by Geneviève LeLoup

Scott Foresman
Reading
Kindergarten

Kindergarten
Wordless Story 9

Seven Sisters
illustrated by
Geneviève LeLoup

Phonics Skill:
• Initial consonant s

Scott Foresman

This book belongs to

_____

Activities for Families: This book gives your child practice with words that begin with s, as in sit. Share the book with your child and together name words you know that have the same sound as sit.

Phonics Skill: Initial consonant s

Seven Sisters

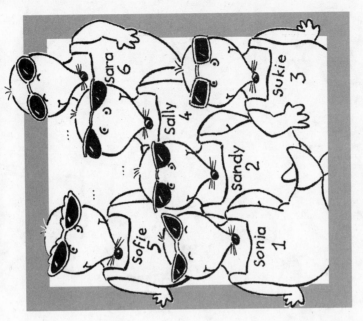

illustrated by Geneviève LeLoup

Scott Foresman

Editorial Offices: Glenview, Illinois • Parsippany, New Jersey • New York, New York
Sales Offices: Parsippany, New Jersey • Duluth, Georgia
Glenview, Illinois • Carrollton, Texas • Ontario, California

© Scott Foresman

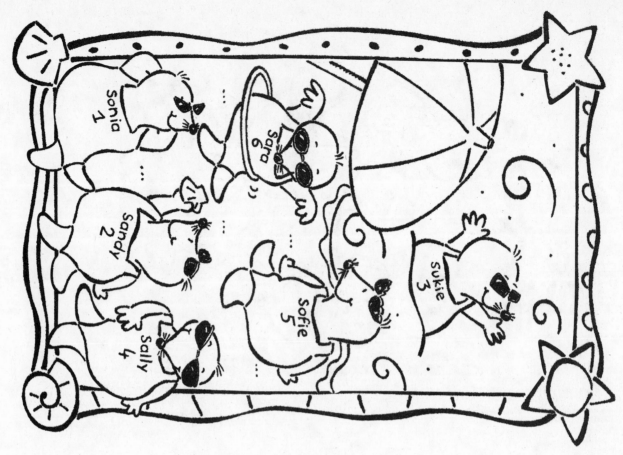

© Scott Foresman

© Scott Foresman

© Scott Foresman

Tom Turkey Gets Wet

illustrated by Valeria Petrone

Scott Foresman Reading
Kindergarten

Kindergarten
Wordless Story 10

Tom Turkey Gets Wet
illustrated by
Valeria Petrone

Phonics Skill:
• Initial and final
  consonant *t*

Scott Foresman

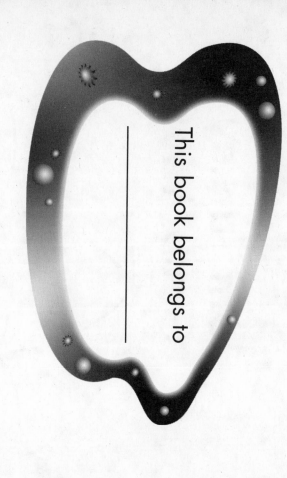

This book belongs to

_____

Activities for Families: This book provides practice with words that begin or end with *t*, as in *Tom* and *wet*. Encourage your child to tell a story using the illustrations in this book. Then find objects in the pictures that begin or end with *t*.

Phonics Skill: Initial and final consonant *t*

Tom Turkey Gets Wet

illustrated by Valeria Petrone

Scott Foresman

Editorial Offices: Glenview, Illinois • Parsippany, New Jersey • New York, New York
Sales Offices: Parsippany, New Jersey • Duluth, Georgia
Glenview, Illinois • Carrollton, Texas • Ontario, California

© Scott Foresman

8

© Scott Foresman

© Scott Foresman

© Scott Foresman

Fifi and Fido

illustrated by Doug Roy

Scott Foresman Reading
Kindergarten

Kindergarten
Wordless Story 11

Fifi and Fido
illustrated by
Doug Roy

Phonics Skill:
• Initial consonant *f*

Scott Foresman

This book belongs to

_____

Activities for Families: This book features things that begin with the *f* sound, as in *Fifi*. Share the book together. Have your child find objects in the pictures that begin with *f*.

Phonics Skill: Initial consonant *f*

Fifi and Fido

illustrated by Doug Roy

Scott Foresman

Editorial Offices: Glenview, Illinois • Parsippany, New Jersey • New York, New York
Sales Offices: Parsippany, New Jersey • Duluth, Georgia
Glenview, Illinois • Carrollton, Texas • Ontario, California

© Scott Foresman

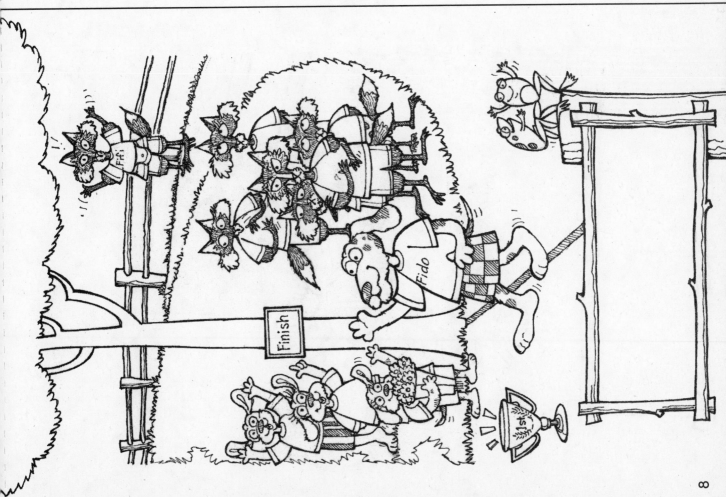

© Scott Foresman

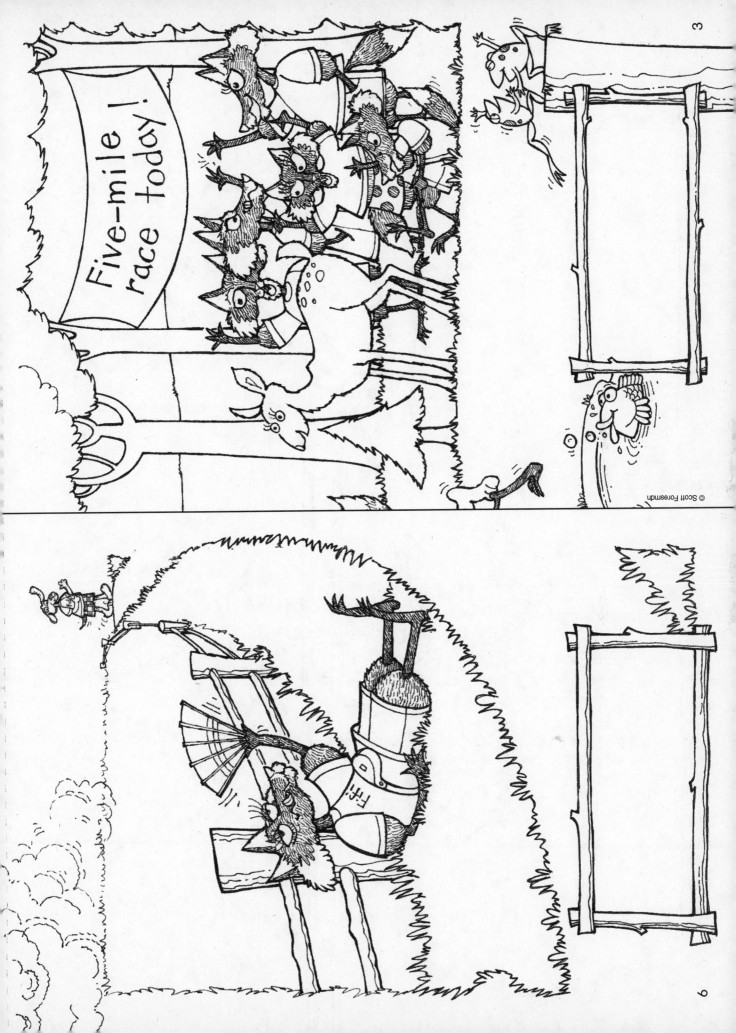

© Scott Foresmdh

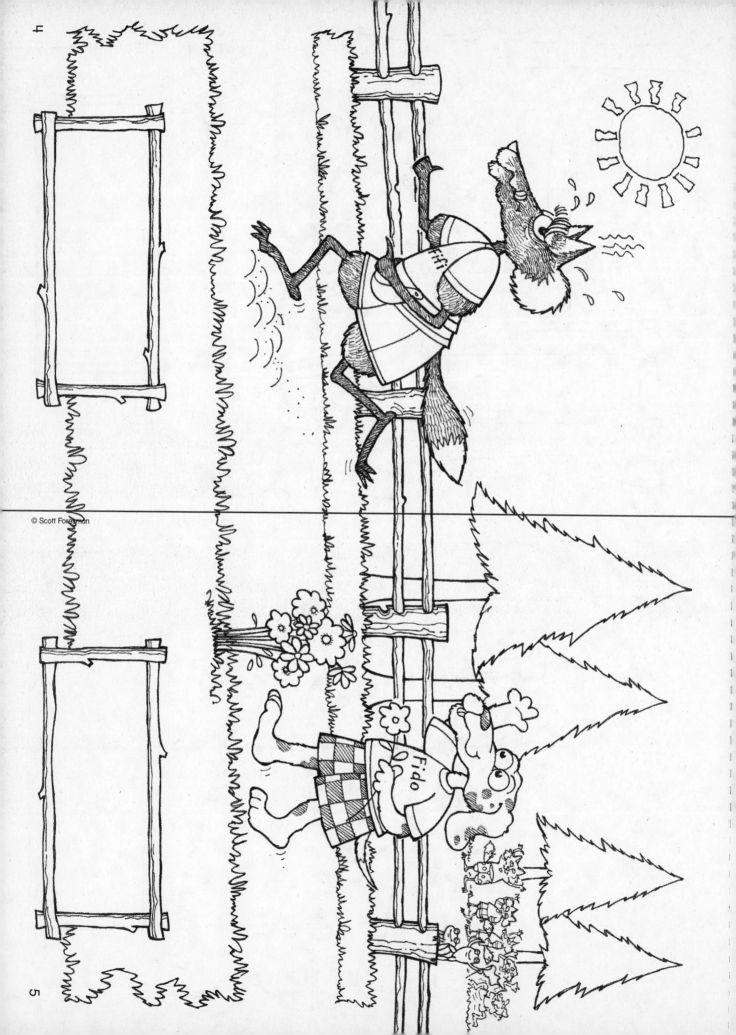

© Scott Foresman

4

5

At Bat

illustrated by Cameron Eagle

Scott Foresman Reading

Kindergarten

Kindergarten
Wordless Story 12

At Bat
illustrated by
Cameron Eagle

Phonics Skill:
• Vowel *a*

Scott Foresman

This book belongs to

_____

Activities for Families: This book gives your child practice with short a words, such as at and rat. After sharing the book, ask your child to name words that rhyme with rat.

Phonics Skill: Vowel a

At Bat

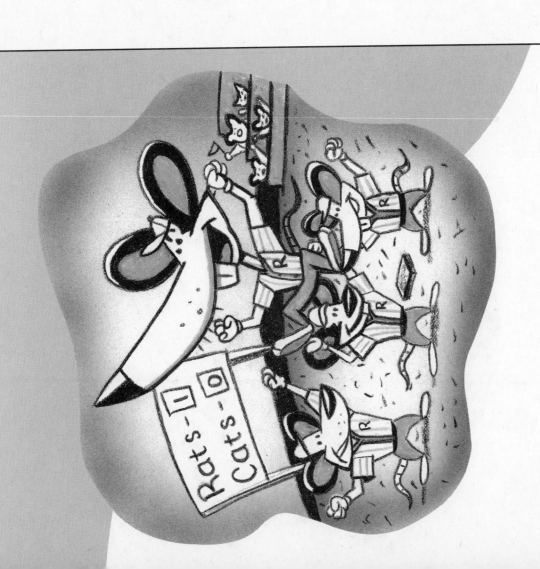

illustrated by Cameron Eagle

Scott Foresman

Editorial Offices: Glenview, Illinois • Parsippany, New Jersey • New York, New York
Sales Offices: Parsippany, New Jersey • Duluth, Georgia
Glenview, Illinois • Carrollton, Texas • Ontario, California

© Scott Foresman

8

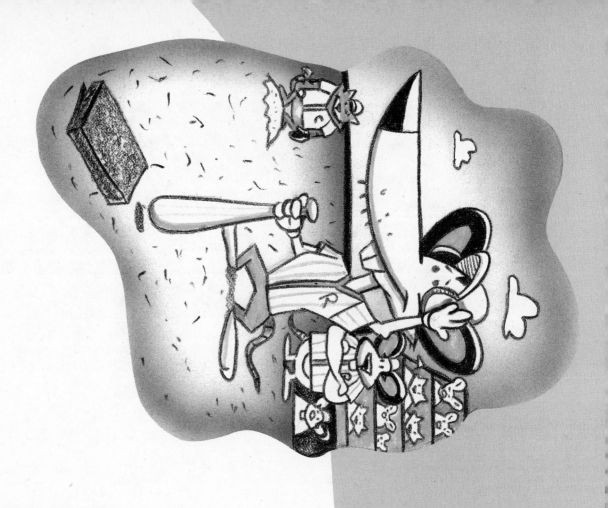

© Scott Foresman

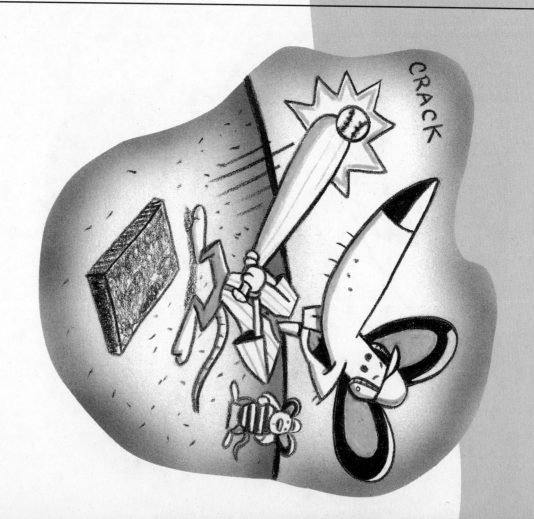

© Scott Foresman

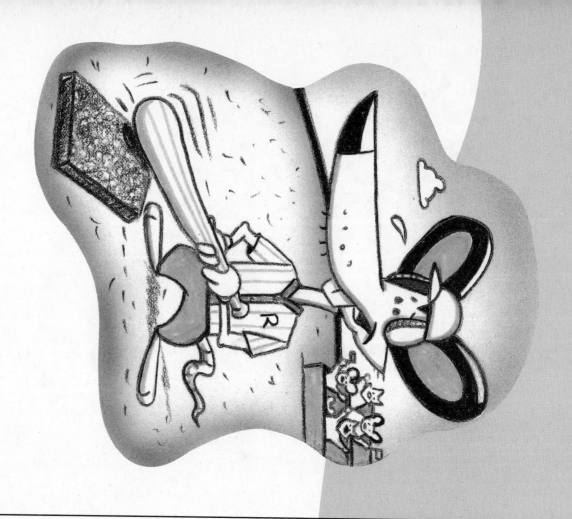

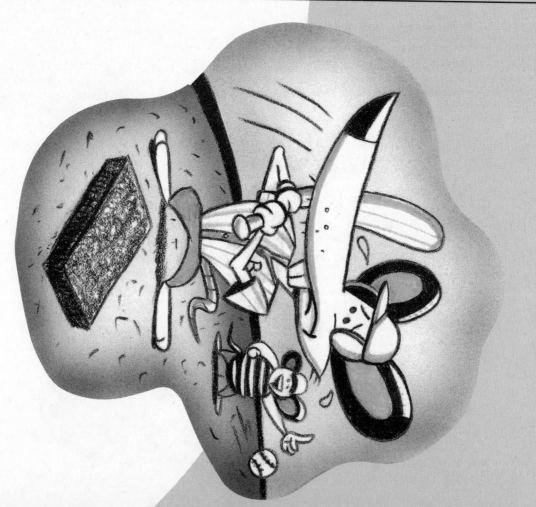

A Cab Ride for Coco

illustrated by David Austin Clar

Scott Foresman **Reading** Kindergarten

Kindergarten
Wordless Story 13

A Cab Ride for Coco
illustrated by
David Austin Clar

Phonics Skill:
• Initial consonant c

Scott Foresman

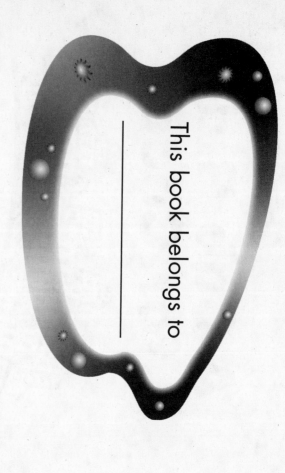

This book belongs to

_____

Activities for Families: Objects that begin with c, such as cab, are featured in this book. Have your child use the illustrations to tell a story and then make up another funny cat story together.

Phonics Skill: Initial consonant c

A Cab Ride for Coco

illustrated by David Austin Clar

Scott Foresman

Editorial Offices: Glenview, Illinois • Parsippany, New Jersey • New York, New York
Sales Offices: Parsippany, New Jersey • Duluth, Georgia
Glenview, Illinois • Carrollton, Texas • Ontario, California

© Scott Foresman

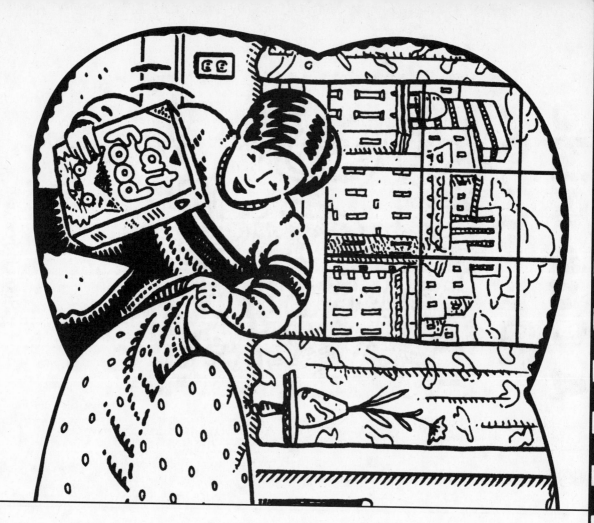

© Scott Foresman

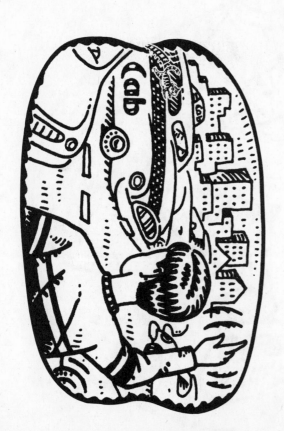 

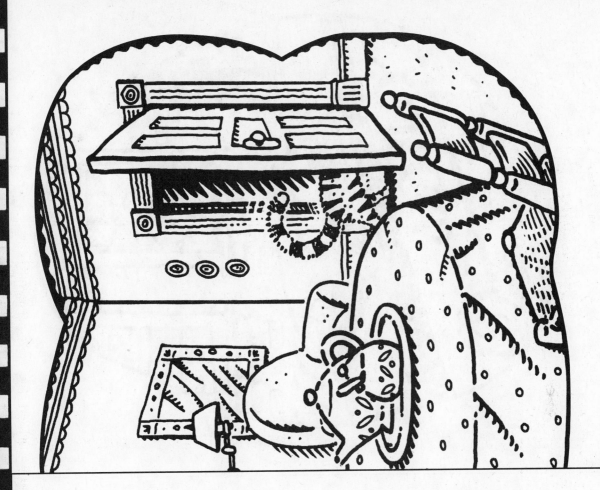

© Scott Foresman

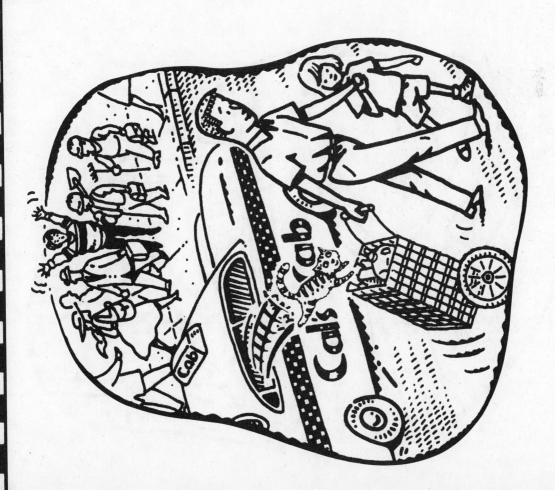

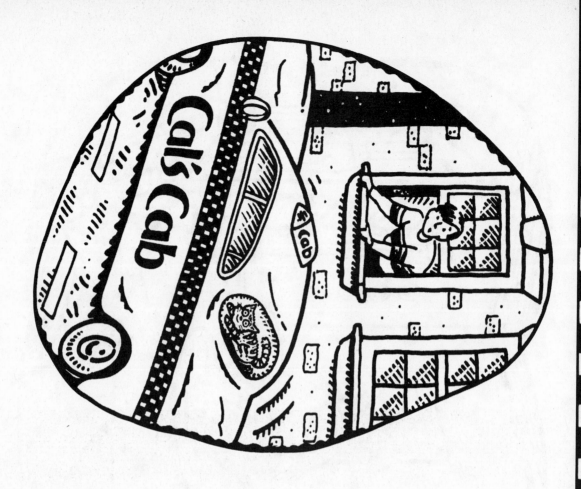

© Scott Foresman

A Prize for Pup

illustrated by Chuck Gonzales

Scott Foresman
Reading
Kindergarten

Kindergarten
Wordless Story 14

A Prize for Pup
illustrated by
Chuck Gonzales

Phonics Skill:
• Initial and final
consonant *p*

Scott Foresman

This book belongs to

_____

Activities for Families: This book features words that begin and end with *p* as in *pig* and *map*. Share the book. Then have your child point out objects in the pictures whose names begin or end with *p*.

Phonics Skill: Initial and final consonant *p*

A Prize for Pup

illustrated by Chuck Gonzales

Scott Foresman

Editorial Offices: Glenview, Illinois • Parsippany, New Jersey • New York, New York
Sales Offices: Parsippany, New Jersey • Duluth, Georgia
Glenview, Illinois • Carrollton, Texas • Ontario, California

© Scott Foresman

© Scott Foresman

© Scott Foresman

© Scott Foresman

No Nap for Ned

illustrated by Mark McIntyre

Scott Foresman Reading
Kindergarten

Kindergarten
Wordless Story 15

No Nap for Ned
illustrated by
Mark McIntyre

Phonics Skill:
• Initial and final
  consonant *n*

Scott Foresman

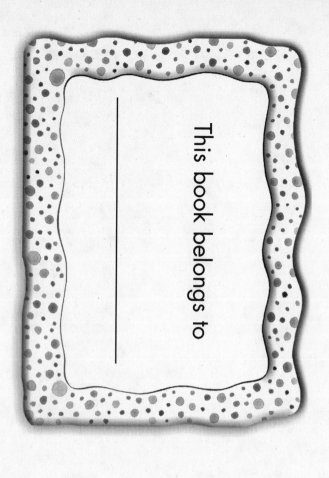

This book belongs to

_____

Activities for Families: This book allows your child to practice words beginning and ending with n, as in *Nan*. After sharing the book, talk about a pet your child has or might like to have.

Phonics Skill: Initial and final consonant n

No Nap for Ned

illustrated by Mark McIntyre

Scott Foresman

Editorial Offices: Glenview, Illinois • Parsippany, New Jersey • New York, New York
Sales Offices: Parsippany, New Jersey • Duluth, Georgia
Glenview, Illinois • Carrollton, Texas • Ontario, California

© Scott Foresman

© Scott Foresman

© Scott Foresman

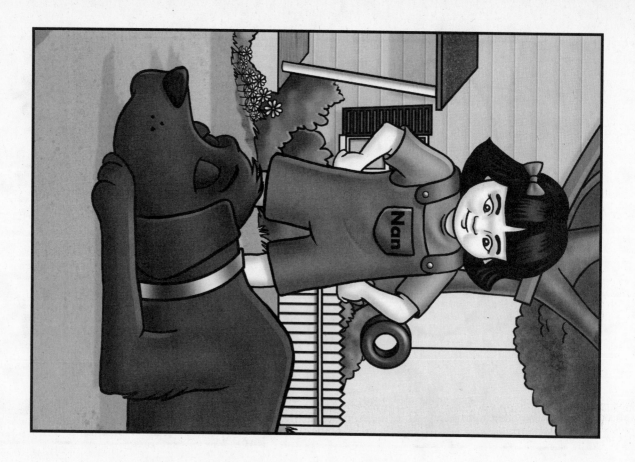

© Scott Foresman

What Is in the Big Rig?

illustrated by Jeff LeVan

Kindergarten
Wordless Story 16

What Is in the Big Rig?
illustrated by
Jeff LeVan

Phonics Skill:
• Vowel *i*

Scott Foresman

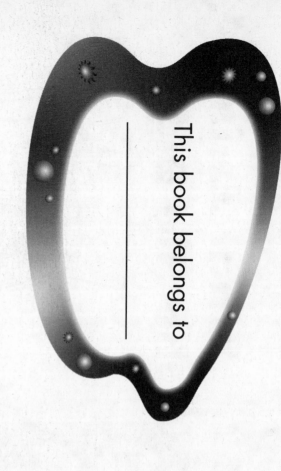

This book belongs to

_____

Activities for Families: This book gives your child practice with short *i* words, such as *big* and *rig*. Have your child use the illustrations in the book to tell a story. Invite your child to name other things that could have been in the big rig.

Phonics Skill: Vowel *i*

What Is in the Big Rig?

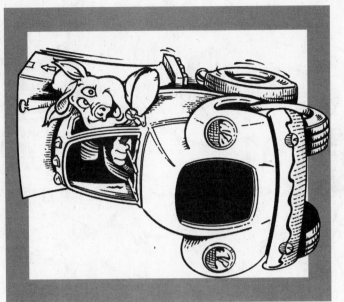

illustrated by Jeff LeVan

Scott Foresman

Editorial Offices: Glenview, Illinois • Parsippany, New Jersey • New York, New York
Sales Offices: Parsippany, New Jersey • Duluth, Georgia
Glenview, Illinois • Carrollton, Texas • Ontario, California

© Scott Foresman

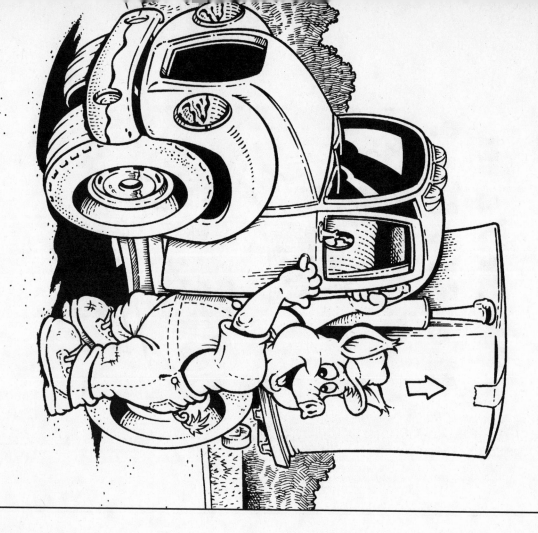

© Scott Foresman

© Scott Foresman

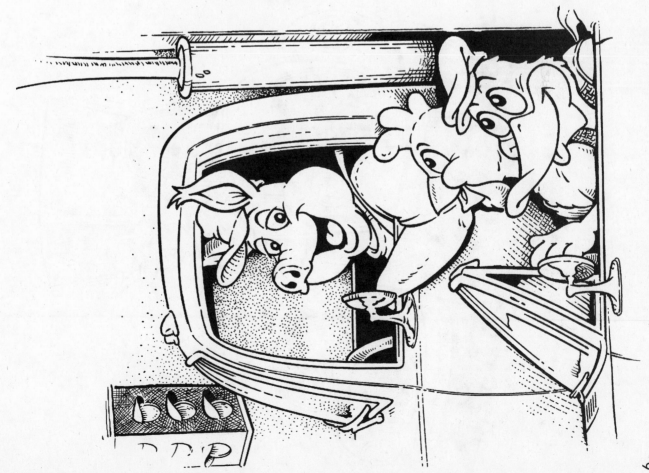

© Scott Foresman

Help on a Hot Day

illustrated by Lisa Chauncy Guida

Scott Foresman
Reading
Kindergarten

Kindergarten
Wordless Story 17

Help on a Hot Day
illustrated by
Lisa Chauncy Guida

Phonics Skill:
• Initial consonant *h*

Scott Foresman

This book belongs to

_____

Activities for Families: This book features objects that begin with *h*, as in *hen*. Have your child use the pictures in this book to tell a story. Then ask him or her to point out things in the pictures that begin with *h*.

Phonics Skill: Initial consonant *h*

Help on a Hot Day

illustrated by Lisa Chauncy Guida

Scott Foresman

Editorial Offices: Glenview, Illinois • Parsippany, New Jersey • New York, New York
Sales Offices: Parsippany, New Jersey • Duluth, Georgia
Glenview, Illinois • Carrollton, Texas • Ontario, California

© Scott Foresman

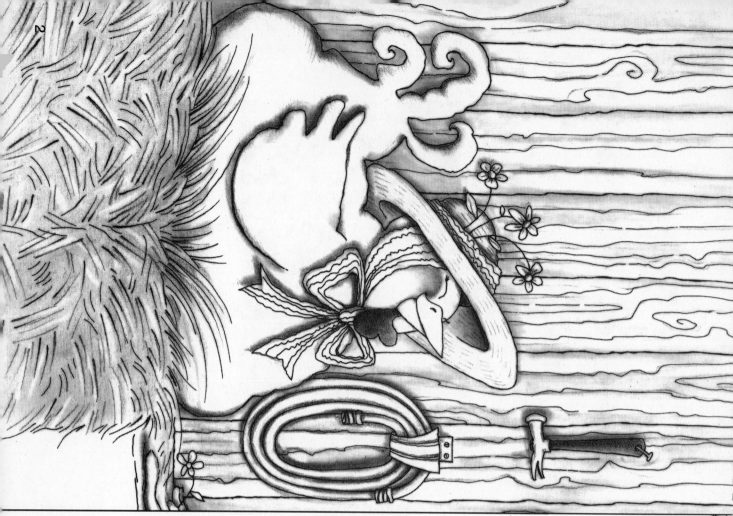

© Scott Foresman

© Scott Foresman

© Scott Foresman

Rosie Rides

illustrated by Dennis Hockerman

Scott Foresman Reading
Kindergarten

Kindergarten
Wordless Story 18

Rosie Rides
illustrated by
Dennis Hockerman

Phonics Skill:
• Initial consonant *r*

Scott Foresman

This book belongs to

_____

Activities for Families: This book gives your child practice with words that begin with *r*, as in *Rosie*. Share the book together. Then search your home for objects whose name begins with the *r* sound.

Phonics Skill: Initial consonant *r*

Rosie Rides

illustrated by Dennis Hockerman

Scott Foresman

Editorial Offices: Glenview, Illinois • Parsippany, New Jersey • New York, New York
Sales Offices: Parsippany, New Jersey • Duluth, Georgia
Glenview, Illinois • Carrollton, Texas • Ontario, California

© Scott Foresman

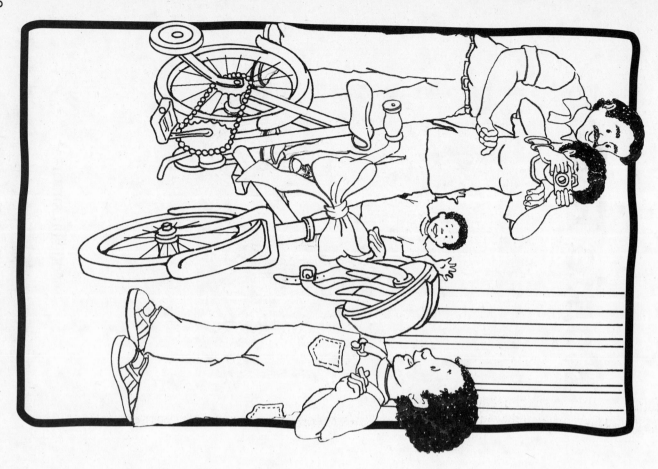

© Scott Foresman

© Scott Foresman

© Scott Foresman

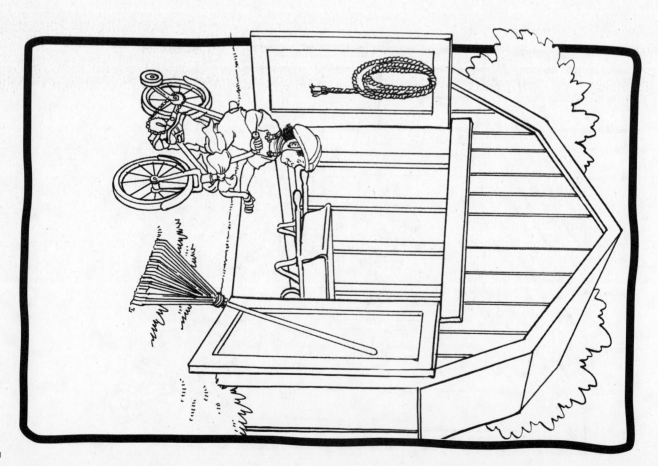

Lemons and Lions

illustrated by Lynn Titleman

Scott Foresman Reading
Kindergarten

Kindergarten
Wordless Story 19

Lemons and Lions
illustrated by
Lynn Titleman

Phonics Skill:
• Initial consonant *l*

Scott Foresman

This book belongs to

_____

Activities for Families: This book features objects whose names begin with *l*, as in *lions*. Encourage your child to tell a story using the illustrations. Then ask him or her to find objects in the illustrations that begin with *l*.

Phonics Skill: Initial consonant *l*

Lemons and Lions

illustrated by Lynn Titleman

Scott Foresman

Editorial Offices: Glenview, Illinois • Parsippany, New Jersey • New York, New York
Sales Offices: Parsippany, New Jersey • Duluth, Georgia
Glenview, Illinois • Carrollton, Texas • Ontario, California

© Scott Foresman

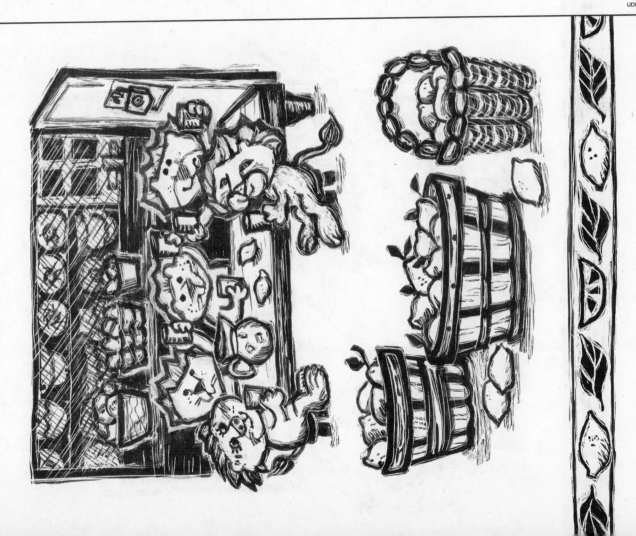

© Scott Foresman

© Scott Foresman

3

6

© Scott Foresman

Dolly Digs!

illustrated by Remy Simard

Scott Foresman Reading
Kindergarten

Kindergarten
Wordless Story 20

Dolly Digs!
illustrated by
Remy Simard

Phonics Skill:
• Initial Consonant d

Scott Foresman

This book belongs to

_____

Activities for Families: This book gives your child practice with words that begin with *d*, as in *Dolly*. Have your child use the pictures to tell a story. Then invite your child to say other names that begin with the *d* sound.

Phonics Skill: Initial consonant *d*

Dolly Digs!

illustrated by Remy Simard

Scott Foresman

Editorial Offices: Glenview, Illinois • Parsippany, New Jersey • New York, New York
Sales Offices: Parsippany, New Jersey • Duluth, Georgia
Glenview, Illinois • Carrollton, Texas • Ontario, California

© Scott Foresman

© Scott Foresman

© Scott Foresman

© Scott Foresman

4

5

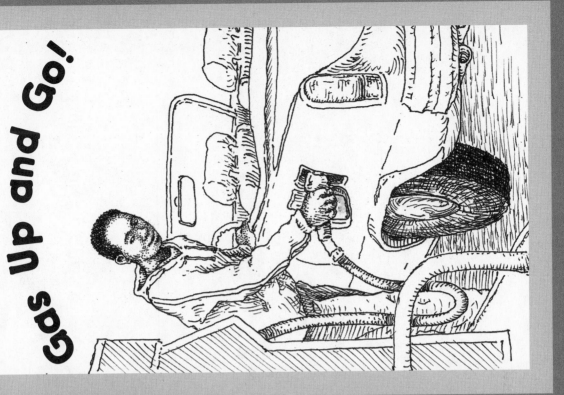

Gas Up and Go!

illustrated by Donald Cook

Scott Foresman Reading
Kindergarten

Kindergarten
Wordless Story 21

Gas Up and Go!
illustrated by
Donald Cook

Phonics Skill:
• Initial and final
  consonant g

Scott Foresman

This book belongs to

_____

Activities for Families: This book gives your child practice with words that begin or end with *g*, as in *gas* or *big*. Share the book together. Invite your child to continue the story by telling what the people in one of the pictures did after leaving the gas station.

Phonics Skill: Initial and final consonant *g*

Gas Up and Go!

illustrated by Donald Cook

Scott Foresman

Editorial Offices: Glenview, Illinois • Parsippany, New Jersey • New York, New York
Sales Offices: Parsippany, New Jersey • Duluth, Georgia
Glenview, Illinois • Carrollton, Texas • Ontario, California

© Scott Foresman

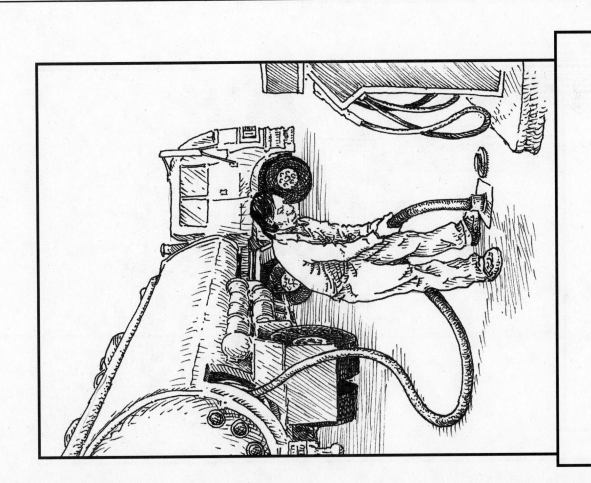

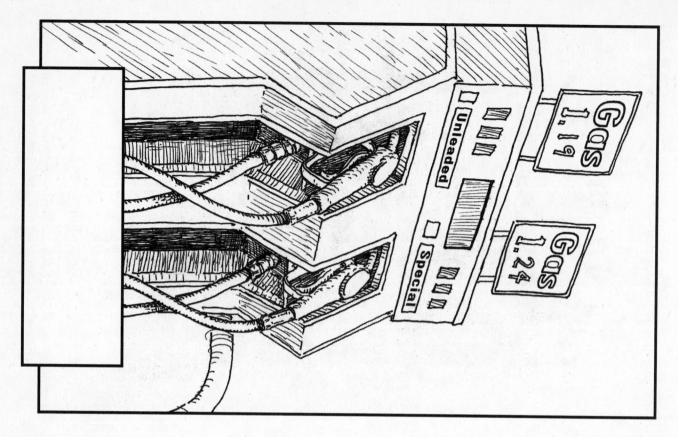

© Scott Foresman

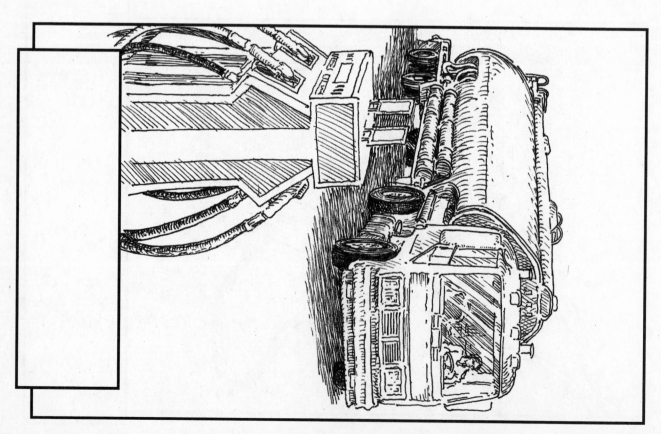

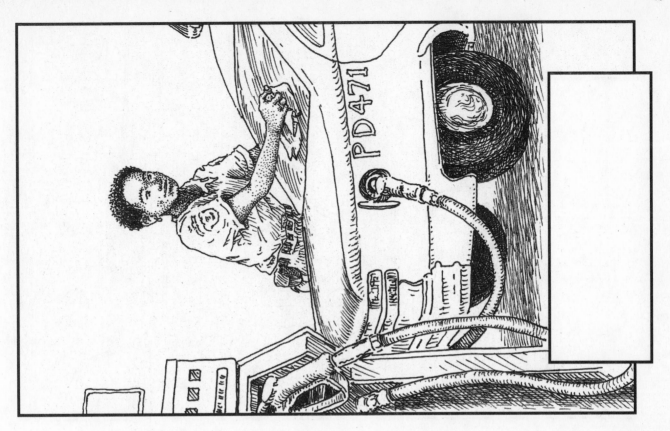

© Scott Foresman

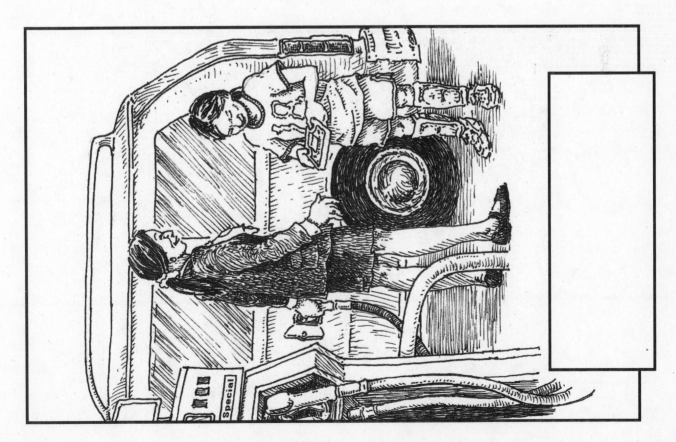

4

© Scott Foresman

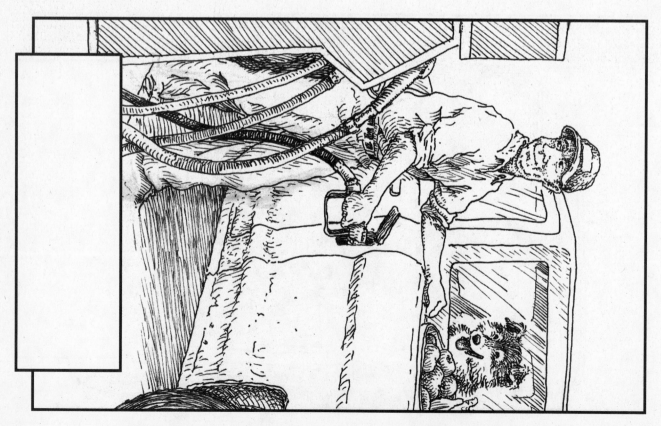

5

Lots and Lots of Dots

illustrated by Dan Vascuncellos

Scott Foresman Reading
Kindergarten

Kindergarten
Wordless Story 22

Lots and Lots of Dots
illustrated by
Dan Vascuncellos

Phonics Skill:
• Vowel o

Scott Foresman

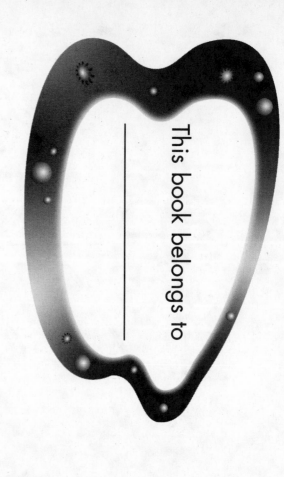

This book belongs to

_____

Activities for Families: This book gives your child practice with short o words, such as *dots*. Share the book and then ask your child to name words that rhyme with *dot*.

Phonics Skill: Vowel o

Lots and Lots of Dots

illustrated by Dan Vascuncellos

Scott Foresman

Editorial Offices: Glenview, Illinois • Parsippany, New Jersey • New York, New York
Sales Offices: Parsippany, New Jersey • Duluth, Georgia
Glenview, Illinois • Carrollton, Texas • Ontario, California

© Scott Foresman

© Scott Foresman

A Bug

© Scott Foresman

© Scott Foresman

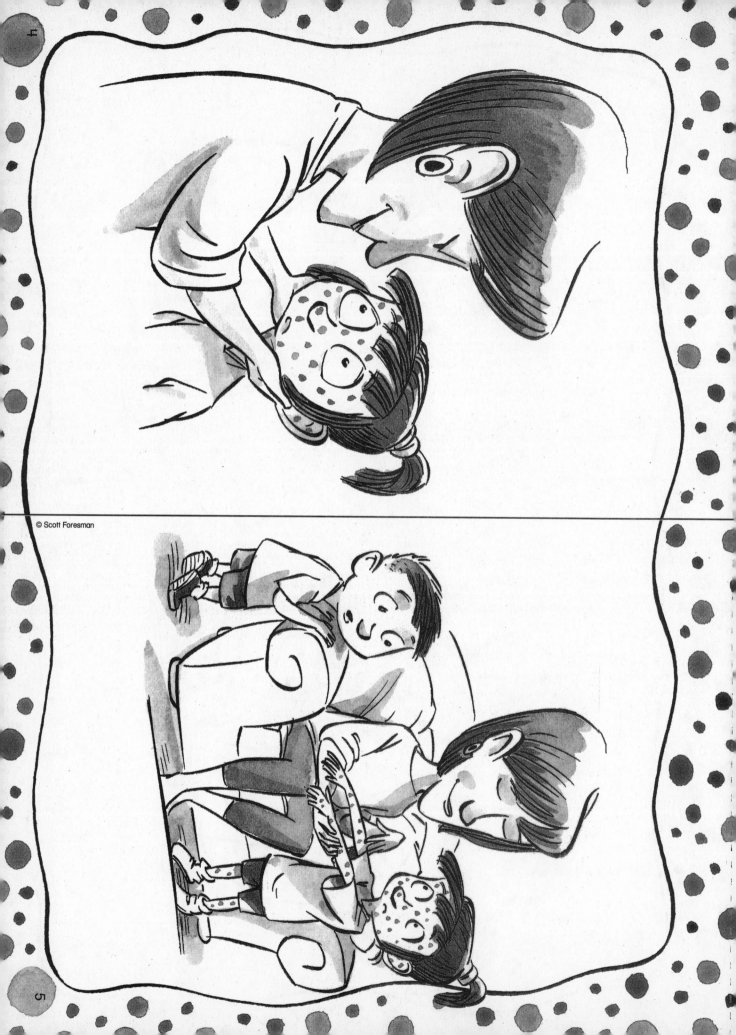

Kids and Kits

Scott Foresman Reading

Kindergarten
Wordless Story 23

Kids and Kits

Phonics Skill:
• Initial consonant *k*

Scott Foresman

This book belongs to

_____

Activities for Families: This book offers practice with words that begin with k, as in kids and kits. Encourage your child to use the pictures to tell a story. Then talk about other names for baby animals.

Phonics Skill: Initial consonant k

Kids and Kits

Scott Foresman

Editorial Offices: Glenview, Illinois • Parsippany, New Jersey • New York, New York
Sales Offices: Parsippany, New Jersey • Duluth, Georgia
Glenview, Illinois • Carrollton, Texas • Ontario, California

© Scott Foresman

8

© Scott Foresman

© Scott Foresman

4

© Scott Foresman

4

5

Wig Is Wet!

illustrated by Paul Harvey

Scott Foresman **Reading**
Kindergarten

Kindergarten
Wordless Story 24

Wig Is Wet!
illustrated by
Paul Harvey

Phonics Skill:
• Initial consonant w

Scott Foresman

This book belongs to

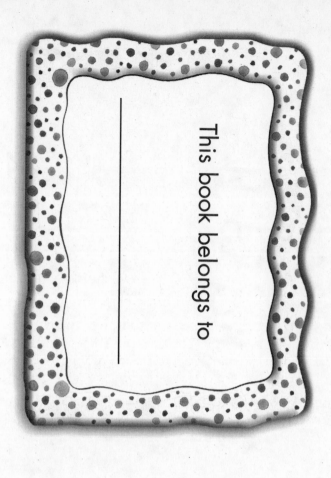

_____

Activities for Families: This book features things that begin with w, as in *Wig*. Invite your child to use the pictures in this book to tell a story. Then take a walk around your home, taking turns naming objects whose names begin with the w sound.

Phonics Skill: Initial consonant w

Wig Is Wet!

illustrated by Paul Harvey

Scott Foresman

Editorial Offices: Glenview, Illinois • Parsippany, New Jersey • New York, New York
Sales Offices: Parsippany, New Jersey • Duluth, Georgia
Glenview, Illinois • Carrollton, Texas • Ontario, California

© Scott Foresman

8

© Scott Foresman

© Scott Foresman

© Scott Foresman

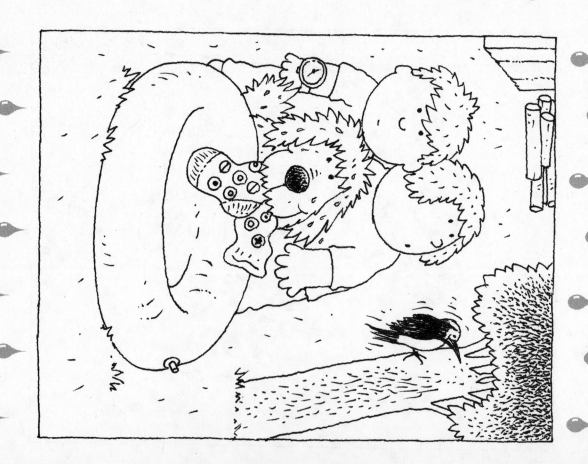

Jelly and Jam

photographed by Richard Hutchings

Scott Foresman

Reading

Kindergarten

Kindergarten
Wordless Story 25

Jelly and Jam
photographed by
Richard Hutchings

Phonics Skill:
• Initial consonant j

Scott Foresman

This book belongs to

_____

Activities for Families: This book offers practice with words that begin with *j*, as in *jelly*. Share the book and then ask your child to think of names for the children that begin with the *j* sound.

Phonics Skill: Initial consonant *j*

Jelly and Jam

photographed by Richard Hutchings

Scott Foresman

Editorial Offices: Glenview, Illinois • Parsippany, New Jersey • New York, New York
Sales Offices: Parsippany, New Jersey • Duluth, Georgia
Glenview, Illinois • Carrollton, Texas • Ontario, California

© Scott Foresman

2

© Scott Foresman

7

© Scott Foresman

4

© Scott Foresman

5

The Van

Move with Vin

illustrated by Rusty Fletcher

Scott Foresman Reading
Kindergarten

Kindergarten
Wordless Story 26

The Van
illustrated by
Rusty Fletcher

Phonics Skill:
• Initial consonant v

Scott Foresman

This book belongs to

_____

Activities for Families: This book gives your child practice in identifying objects that begin with v, as in *van*. Share the book and then encourage your child to find objects in the pictures whose names begin with v.

Phonics Skill: Initial consonant v

The Van

illustrated by Rusty Fletcher

Scott Foresman

Editorial Offices: Glenview, Illinois • Parsippany, New Jersey • New York, New York
Sales Offices: Parsippany, New Jersey • Duluth, Georgia
Glenview, Illinois • Carrollton, Texas • Ontario, California

© Scott Foresman

© Scott Foresman

© Scott Foresman

© Scott Foresman

4

5

The Queen
and
the Quilt

illustrated by Luisa D'Augusta

Scott Foresman
Reading
Kindergarten

Kindergarten
Wordless Story 27

The Queen
and the Quilt
illustrated by
Luisa D'Augusta

Phonics Skill:
• Initial consonant q

Scott Foresman

This book belongs to

_____

Activities for Families: This book provides practice with words that have the same beginning sound as *queen*. Invite your child to use the illustrations to tell a story. Then help them point out objects in the book that begin with *qu*.

Phonics Skill: Initial consonant *q*

The Queen and the Quilt

illustrated by Luisa D'Augusta

Scott Foresman

Editorial Offices: Glenview, Illinois • Parsippany, New Jersey • New York, New York
Sales Offices: Parsippany, New Jersey • Duluth, Georgia
Glenview, Illinois • Carrollton, Texas • Ontario, California

© Scott Foresman

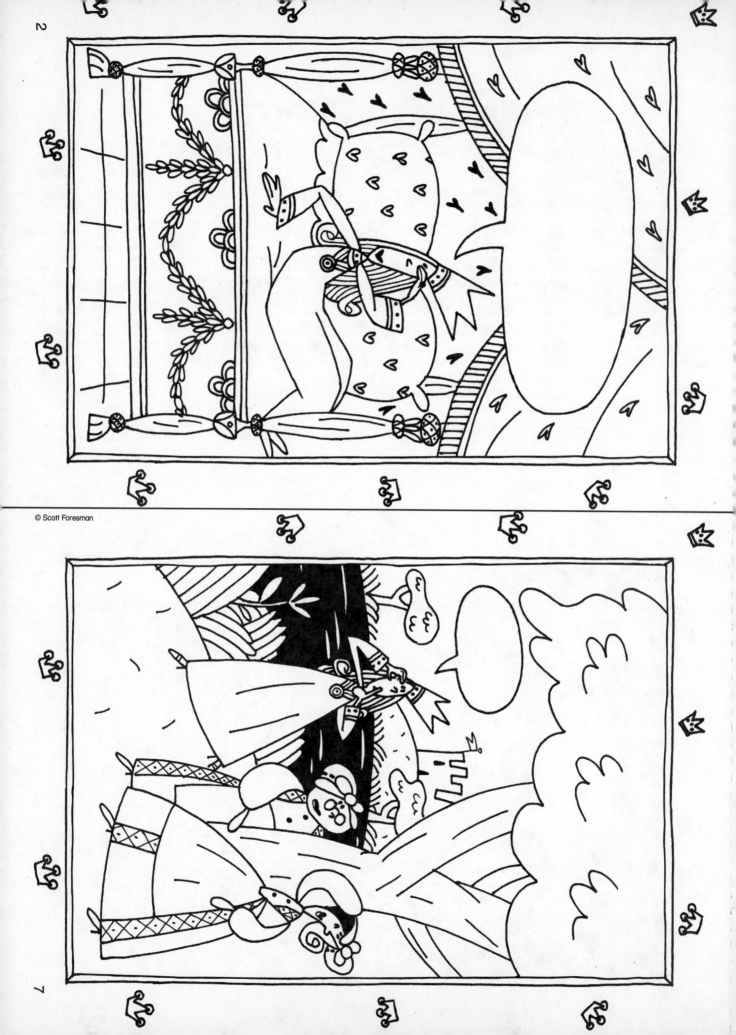

© Scott Foresman

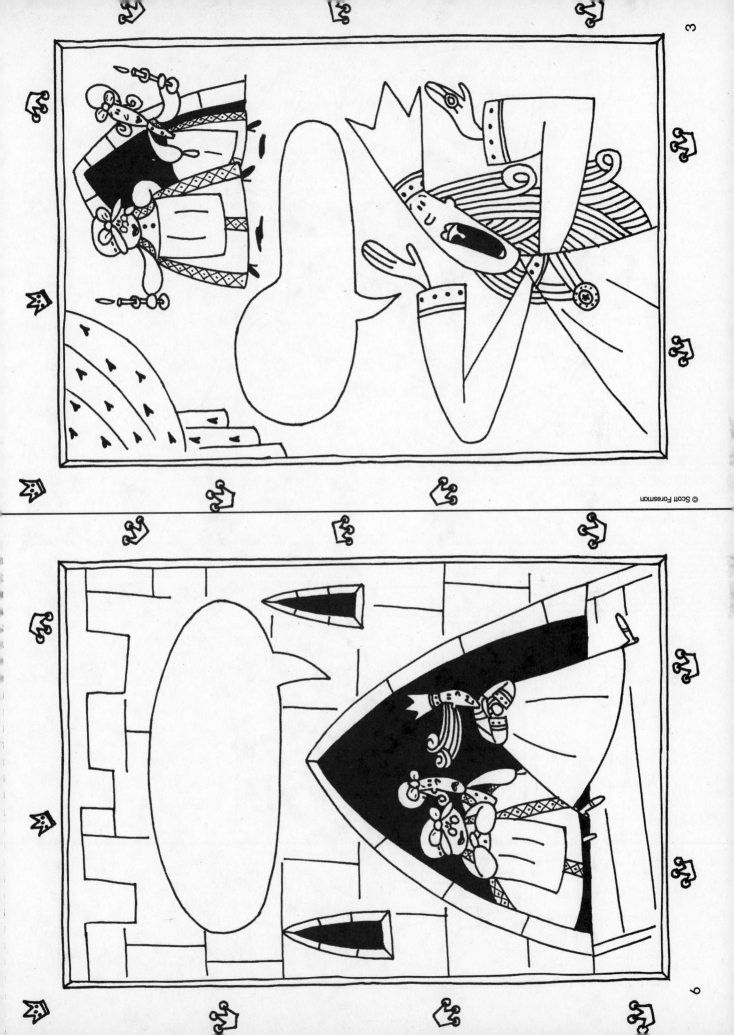

© Scott Foresman

3

6

© Scott Foresman

Em, Ed, and Jet

illustrated by Jackie Urbanovic

Scott Foresman Reading Kindergarten

Kindergarten
Wordless Story 28

Em, Ed, and Jet
illustrated by
Jackie Urbanovic

Phonics Skill:
• Vowel e

Scott Foresman

This book belongs to

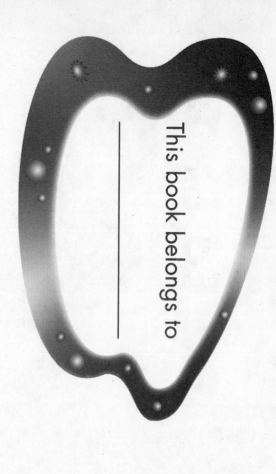

_____

Activities for Families: This book gives your child practice with short e words such as *Ed* and *Jet*. Have your child use the pictures to tell a story. Then together, name words that rhyme with *Ed* or *Jet*.

Phonics Skill: Vowel e

Em, Ed, and Jet

illustrated by Jackie Urbanovic

Scott Foresman

Editorial Offices: Glenview, Illinois • Parsippany, New Jersey • New York, New York
Sales Offices: Parsippany, New Jersey • Duluth, Georgia
Glenview, Illinois • Carrollton, Texas • Ontario, California

© Scott Foresman

2

© Scott Foresman

© Scott Foresman

3

6

4

© Scott Foresman

5

Six Monkeys

illustrated by Tim Haggerty

Scott Foresman Reading

Kindergarten

Kindergarten
Wordless Story 29

Six Monkeys
illustrated by
Tim Haggerty

Phonics Skill:
• Initial and final
consonant x

Scott Foresman

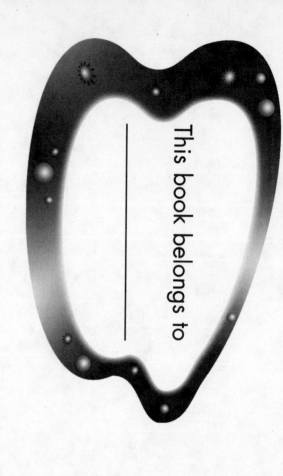

This book belongs to

_____

Activities for Families: This book gives your child practice with words containing x, such as six. Encourage your child to tell a story using the pictures. Go back through the book and find objects whose names contain an x.

Phonics Skill: Initial and final consonant x

Six Monkeys

illustrated by Tim Haggerty

Scott Foresman

Editorial Offices: Glenview, Illinois • Parsippany, New Jersey • New York, New York
Sales Offices: Parsippany, New Jersey • Duluth, Georgia
Glenview, Illinois • Carrollton, Texas • Ontario, California

© Scott Foresman

© Scott Foresman

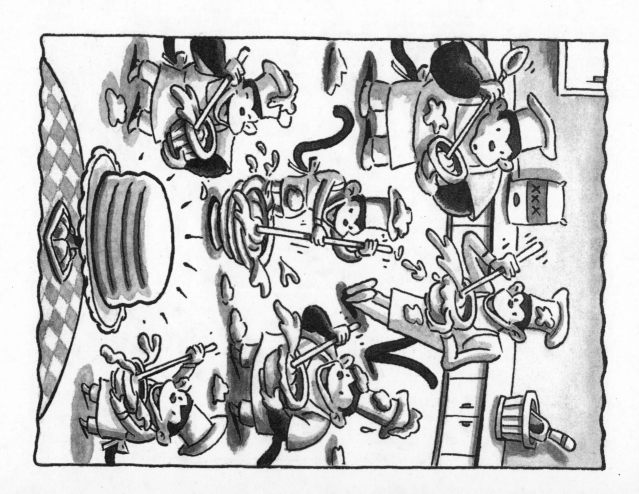

© Scott Foresman

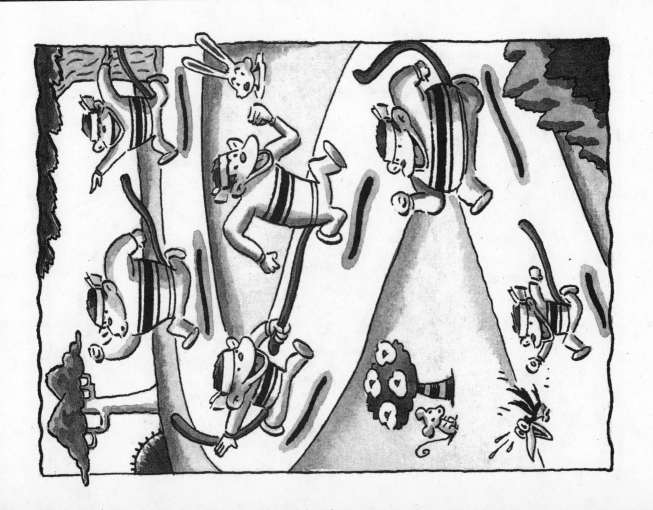

© Scott Foresman

Yoki and Yum Yum

illustrated by John Margeson

Scott Foresman
Reading
Kindergarten

Kindergarten
Wordless Story 30

Yoki and Yum Yum
illustrated by
John Margeson

Phonics Skill:
• Initial consonant y

Scott Foresman

This book belongs to

_____

Activities for Families: This book provides practice with words that begin with y, such as *Yoki*. After sharing the book together, encourage your child to suggest things he or she might make with a large box.

Phonics Skill: Initial consonant y

Yoki and Yum Yum

illustrated by John Margeson

Scott Foresman

Editorial Offices: Glenview, Illinois • Parsippany, New Jersey • New York, New York
Sales Offices: Parsippany, New Jersey • Duluth, Georgia
Glenview, Illinois • Carrollton, Texas • Ontario, California

© Scott Foresman

© Scott Foresman

© Scott Foresman

© Scott Foresman

Zebra
Hears a Buzz

illustrated by Eldon Doty

Scott Foresman Reading
Kindergarten

Kindergarten
Wordless Story 31

Zebra Hears a Buzz
illustrated by
Eldon Doty

Phonics Skill:
• Initial and final
  consonant z

Scott Foresman

This book belongs to

_____

Activities for Families: This book provides practice with words that begin or end with z, as in *zebra* and *buzz*. Have your child tell a story using the illustrations. Invite your child to think of other animals found in a zoo.

Phonics Skill: Initial and final consonant z

Zebra
Hears a Buzz

illustrated by Eldon Doty

Scott Foresman

Editorial Offices: Glenview, Illinois • Parsippany, New Jersey • New York, New York
Sales Offices: Parsippany, New Jersey • Duluth, Georgia
Glenview, Illinois • Carrollton, Texas • Ontario, California

© Scott Foresman

8

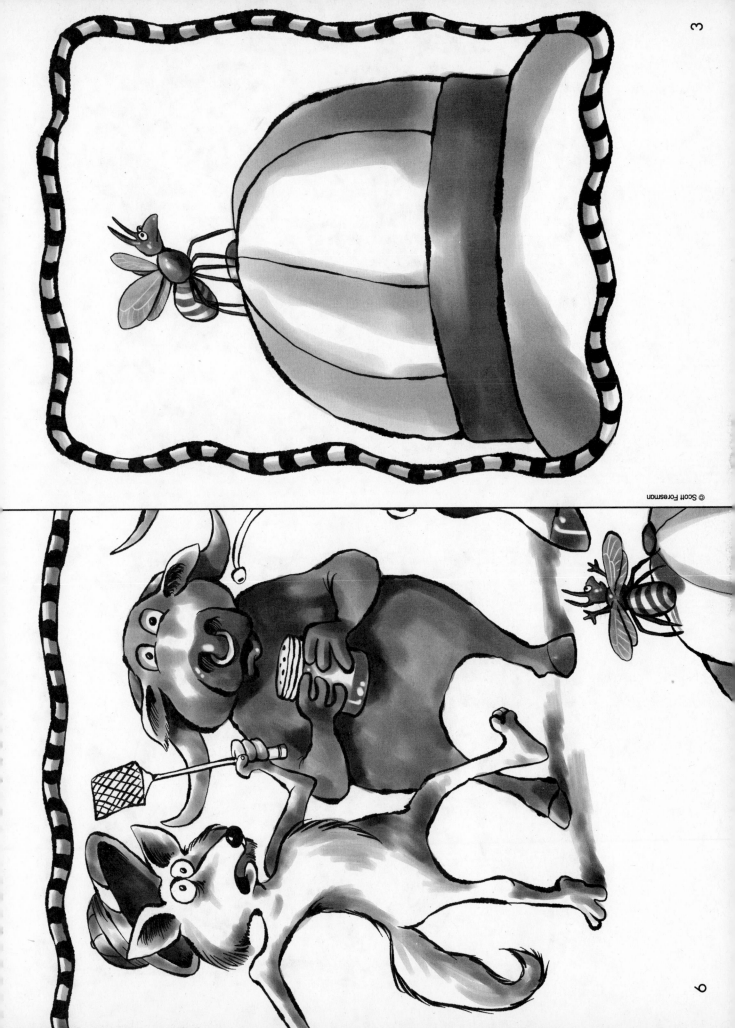

© Scott Foresman

© Scott Foresman

Bugs! Bugs! Bugs!

illustrated by Andrea Tachiera

Scott Foresman Reading
Kindergarten

Kindergarten
Wordless Story 32

Bugs! Bugs! Bugs!
illustrated by
Andrea Tachiera

Phonics Skill:
• Vowel *u*

Scott Foresman

This book belongs to

_____

Activities for Families: The book gives your child practice with short *u* words, such as *bugs*. Invite your child to tell a story using the pictures. Then together, make up rhymes with the short *u* words. Example: *A bug is under the rug.*

Phonics Skill: Vowel *u*

Bugs! Bugs! Bugs!

illustrated by Andrea Tachiera

Scott Foresman

Editorial Offices: Glenview, Illinois • Parsippany, New Jersey • New York, New York
Sales Offices: Parsippany, New Jersey • Duluth, Georgia
Glenview, Illinois • Carrollton, Texas • Ontario, California

© Scott Foresman

Bug Hut

© Scott Foresman

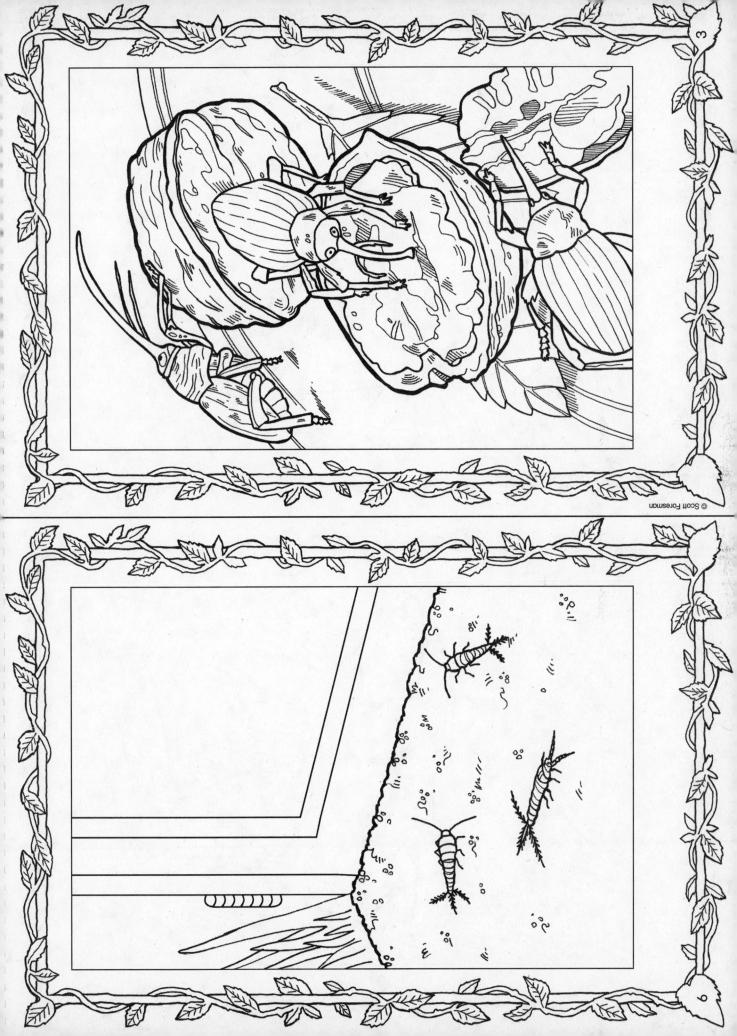

© Scott Foresman

© Scott Foresman

Running on a Sandy Beach

illustrated by Abby Carter

Scott Foresman **Reading**
Kindergarten

Kindergarten
Wordless Story 33

Running on a
Sandy Beach
illustrated by Abby Carter

Phonics Review:
• Consonants

Scott Foresman

This book belongs to

_____

Activities for Families: This book offers a review of consonants. Share the book and then encourage your child to think of other things to do on a sandy beach.

Phonics Review: Consonants

Running on a Sandy Beach

illustrated by Abby Carter

Scott Foresman

Editorial Offices: Glenview, Illinois • Parsippany, New Jersey • New York, New York
Sales Offices: Parsippany, New Jersey • Duluth, Georgia
Glenview, Illinois • Carrollton, Texas • Ontario, California

© Scott Foresman

8

© Scott Foresman

© Scott Foresman

3

6

© Scott Foresman

Hat in the Grass

Grass

illustrated by Esther Szegedy

Scott Foresman Reading
Kindergarten

Kindergarten
Wordless Story 34

Hat in the Grass
illustrated by
Esther Szegedy

Phonics Skill:
• Initial consonant blends

Scott Foresman

This book belongs to

_____

Activities for Families: This book gives your child practice with words that begin with consonant blends, such as *grass*. Encourage your child to use the illustrations to tell a story. Then together, find objects in your home whose names begin with a consonant blend.

Phonics Skill: Initial consonant blends

Hat in the Grass

illustrated by Esther Szegedy

Scott Foresman

Editorial Offices: Glenview, Illinois • Parsippany, New Jersey • New York, New York
Sales Offices: Parsippany, New Jersey • Duluth, Georgia
Glenview, Illinois • Carrollton, Texas • Ontario, California

© Scott Foresman

8

© Scott Foresman

© Scott Foresman

Uncle Piggy Shops

illustrated by Randy Verougstraet

Scott Foresman Reading Kindergarten

Kindergarten
Wordless Story 35

Uncle Piggy Shops
illustrated by
Randy Verougstraet

Phonics Review:
• Short vowels

Scott Foresman

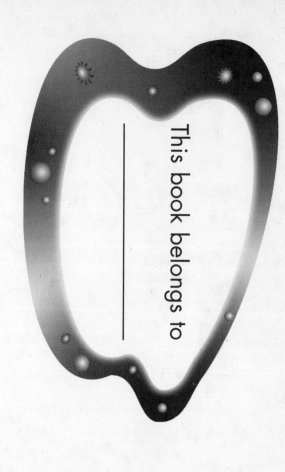

This book belongs to

_____

Activities for Families: This book offers a review of short vowels. Have your child tell a story using the illustrations. Invite your child to name places he or she likes to shop.

Phonics Review: Short vowels

Uncle Piggy Shops

illustrated by Randy Verougstraet

Scott Foresman

Editorial Offices: Glenview, Illinois • Parsippany, New Jersey • New York, New York
Sales Offices: Parsippany, New Jersey • Duluth, Georgia
Glenview, Illinois • Carrollton, Texas • Ontario, California

© Scott Foresman

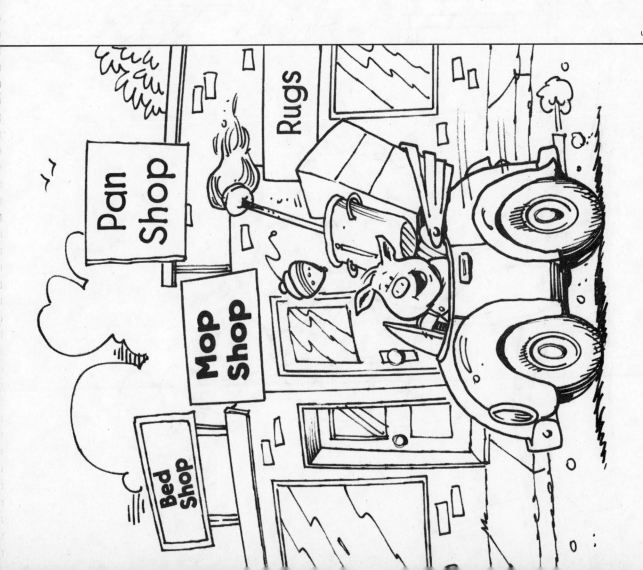

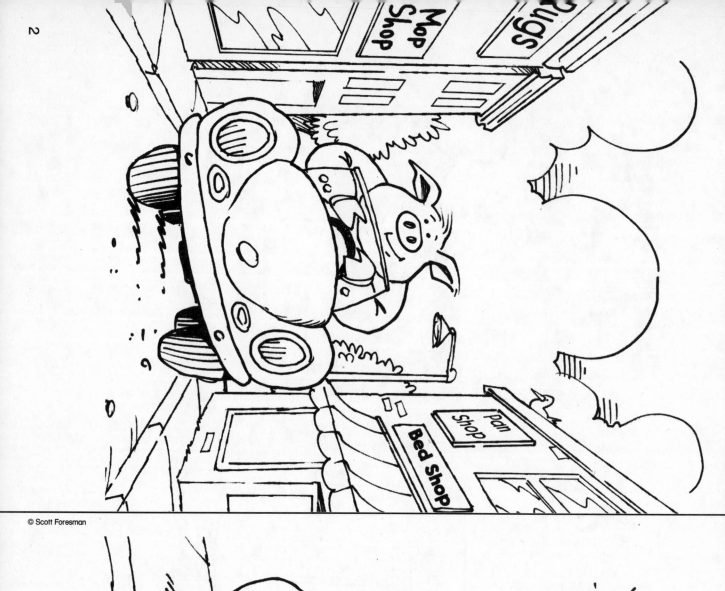

© Scott Foresman

© Scott Foresman

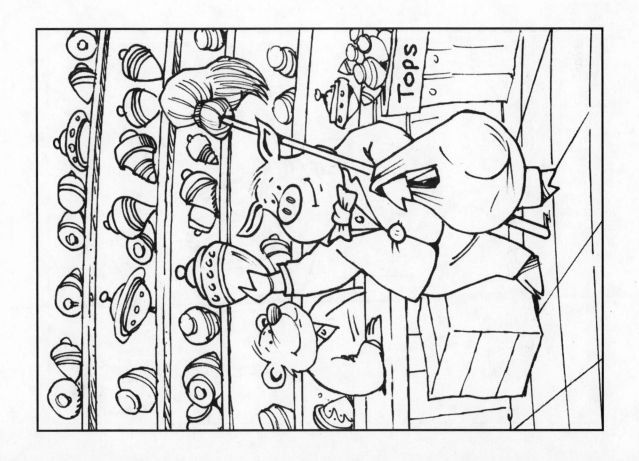

Tops

© Scott Foresman

Sharks

illustrated by Jon Weiman

Scott Foresman
Reading
Kindergarten

**Kindergarten
Wordless Story 36**

Sharks
illustrated by
Jon Weiman

Phonics Review:
• Consonants
• Short vowels

Scott Foresman

This book belongs to

_____

Activities for Families: This book provides a review of consonants and short vowels. Encourage your child to tell a story using the illustrations in this book. Then together name and talk about other animals that live in the sea.

Phonics Review: Consonants; Short vowels

Sharks

illustrated by Jon Weiman

Scott Foresman

Editorial Offices: Glenview, Illinois • Parsippany, New Jersey • New York, New York
Sales Offices: Parsippany, New Jersey • Duluth, Georgia
Glenview, Illinois • Carrollton, Texas • Ontario, California

© Scott Foresman

2

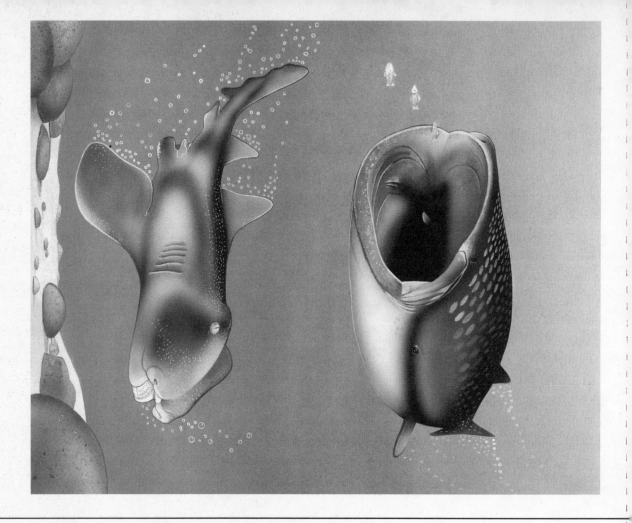

© Scott Foresman

7

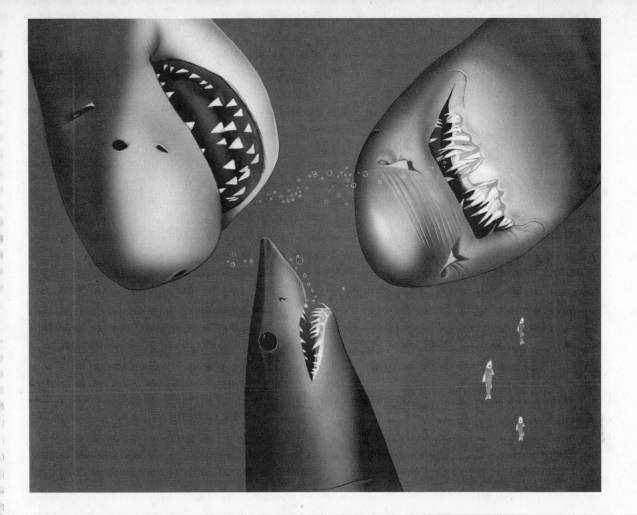

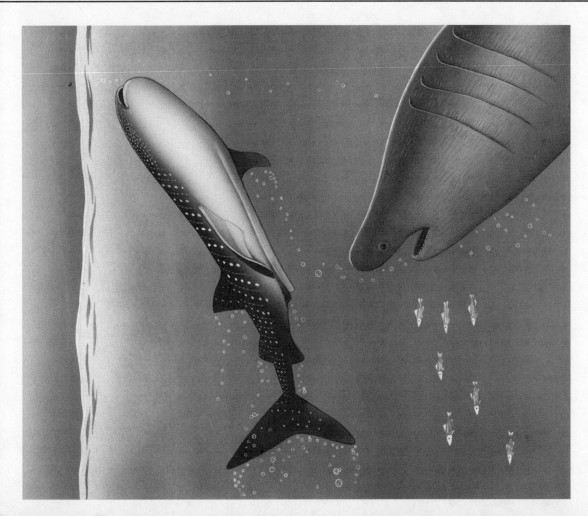

Foresman

© Scott Foresman

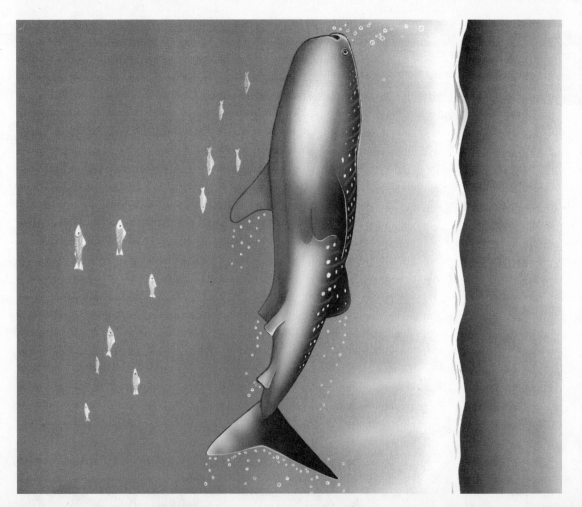